First Facts®

EXTREME PLANET

THE WETTEST PLACES ON EARTH

by Martha E. H. Rustad

Consultant:
Randall S. Cerveny, PhD
President's Professor, School of Geographical Sciences
Arizona State University, Tempe

CAPSTONE PRESS
a capstone imprint

First Facts is published by Capstone Press,
151 Good Counsel Drive, P.O. Box 669, Mankato, Minnesota 56002.
www.capstonepress.com

092009
005618CGS10

 Books published by Capstone Press are manufactured with paper
containing at least 10 percent post-consumer waste.

Library of Congress Cataloging-in-Publication Data
Rustad, Martha E. H. (Martha Elizabeth Hillman), 1975–
    The wettest places on Earth / by Martha E. H. Rustad.
    p. cm. — (First facts. Extreme planet)
    Summary: "An introduction to the wettest places on Earth, including maps and colorful
photographs" — Provided by publisher.
    Includes bibliographical references and index.
    ISBN 978-1-4296-3966-8 (library binding)
    1. Climatic extremes — Juvenile literature. 2. Rain and rainfall — Juvenile literature.
3. Tropics — Climate — Juvenile literature. I. Title. II. Series.
QC981.8.C53R875 2010
551.57'7 — dc22
                                                        2009026041

Editorial credits
Erika L. Shores, editor; Ted Williams, designer; Svetlana Zhurkin, media researcher;
    Eric Manske, production specialist

Photo credits
Alamy/Keith Erskine, 16; Roger Fletcher, 21
Corbis/Buddy Mays, cover; epa, 19
David Vaucher, 13
Newscom, 10
Photolibrary/Pacific Stock/Abraham Bob, 7
Sebastian Todt, 9
Shutterstock/Lijuan Guo, 15; Marc van Vuren, 5

Essential content terms are **bold** and are defined at the bottom of the spread where they first appear.

TABLE OF CONTENTS

SOAKING WET

Imagine living in the wettest places on earth. You might need an umbrella every day. Hundreds of inches of **precipitation** fall in these wet spots. People measure the rain, hail, sleet, or snow that falls from clouds. Let's explore some of earth's soggiest places.

> **precipitation** — water that falls from clouds to the earth's surface in the form of rain, hail, sleet, or snow

8 PAGO PAGO, AMERICAN SAMOA

Each year, about 119 inches (302 centimeters) of rain soaks the town of Pago Pago, American Samoa. In this U.S. territory, the rainy season lasts from November to April. But it's warm and humid year-round in American Samoa. Temperatures can reach 90 degrees Fahrenheit (32 degrees Celsius).

humid — damp and moist

PAGO PAGO, AMERICAN SAMOA

N
W · E
S

7

7 LAE, PAPUA NEW GUINEA

Warm, wet weather lasts all year in Lae, Papua New Guinea. About 183 inches (465 centimeters) of rain falls each year in this city. Every month, about 20 days are wet and rainy.

EXTREME FACT!

People build houses on stilts in parts of Papua New Guinea. When heavy rains fall, floodwater flows under the houses.

LAE, PAPUA NEW GUINEA

N
W E
S

MOULMEIN, MYANMAR

EXTREME FACT!

The Asian monsoon creates a rainy region that stretches from China to eastern Africa.

MOULMEIN, MYANMAR

The monsoon brings rain to Moulmein, Myanmar, every year. About 190 inches (480 centimeters) of rain falls from June to September. Strong ocean winds bring rain to land during the monsoon. Little rain falls in Moulmein the rest of the year.

monsoon — a season where strong ocean winds bring rain to inland areas

5 MONROVIA, LIBERIA

From April to November, rain falls almost daily in Monrovia, Liberia. Each year, the rainfall adds up to about 202 inches (513 centimeters). But from December to March, a dry desert wind blows through Monrovia. Only about 12 inches (30 centimeters) of rain falls in those months.

MONROVIA, LIBERIA

4 MOUNT BAKER

Imagine a 10-story building made of snow. Now imagine that snow in your backyard. During the winter of 1998 to 1999, 1,140 inches (2,896 centimeters) of snow fell at Mount Baker in Washington. It set a U.S. record for the most snowfall in one season.

MOUNT BAKER, WASHINGTON

FOC-FOC RÉUNION ISLAND

N
W E
S

FOC-FOC, RÉUNION ISLAND

3

The wettest day ever recorded happened in an area called Foc-Foc. A tropical cyclone hit this area of Réunion Island. In January 1966, 72 inches (183 centimeters) of rain fell in one 24-hour period.

cyclone — a storm with strong winds that blow around a center

2 CHERRAPUNJI, INDIA

Each year, the monsoon soaks Cherrapunji, India, with about 450 inches (1,143 centimeters) of rain. Between August 1860 and July 1861, 1,042 inches (2,647 centimeters) of rain fell. That rainfall set a world record.

The rain that falls on Cherrapunji runs down steep hills surrounding the city. People can't store enough water to meet their needs. They must buy water from nearby places.

CHERRAPUNJI, INDIA

1 MOUNT WAIALEALE

Mount Waialeale is an inactive volcano on the Hawaiian island of Kauai. Warm, tropical winds push moisture up the mountain, causing heavy rains. Average yearly rainfall tops 460 inches (1,168 centimeters). All that rain makes Mount Waialeale the rainiest spot on earth.

Many trees and plants cover Mount Waialeale. They grow well in the warm, wet climate.

EXTREME FACT!

MOUNT WAIALEALE

GLOSSARY

cyclone (SYE-klone) — a storm with strong winds that blow around a center; cyclones are also called hurricanes or typhoons.

humid (HYOO-mid) — damp and moist

monsoon (mon-SOON) — a season where strong ocean winds bring rain to inland areas

precipitation (pri-sip-i-TAY-shuhn) — water that falls from clouds to the earth's surface in the form of rain, hail, sleet, or snow

territory (TER-uh-tor-ee) — an area under the control of a country

volcano (vol-KAY-noh) — a mountain with vents from which lava, ash, and gas erupt

READ MORE

Birch, Robin. *How Weather Works.* Weather and Climate. New York: Marshall Cavendish Benchmark, 2009.

Hirschmann, Kris. *It's Wet Out!* What's It Like Out? Edina, Minn.: Abdo, 2008.

Rodgers, Alan and Angella Streluk. *Precipitation.* Measuring the Weather. Chicago: Heinemann, 2007.

INTERNET SITES

FactHound offers a safe, fun way to find Internet sites related to this book. All of the sites on FactHound have been researched by our staff.

Here's all you do:

Visit *www.facthound.com*

FactHound will fetch the best sites for you!

INDEX